Tabby's Guide to Thoughtful Tea Drinking

Written by Tabby (& Michael Gorzka)

Cover design by Dinora Nurtdinova

Interior illustrations by Tanya Zeinalova and Henry Viera

The publisher (and Tabby) advises readers to take full responsibility for their technology use and have neither liability nor responsibility to any person or entity with respect to any loss or damages arising from the information contained in this book.

Table of Contents

YOU CAN'T BUY HAPPINESS
BUT YOU CAN
BUY TEA
AND THAT'S KIND
OF THE SAME THING

Preface: Use of Italics

Any *italicized* words or phrases you see in this book will be subjects of Help for the Technology Shy how-to videos and short articles (i.e. blog posts).

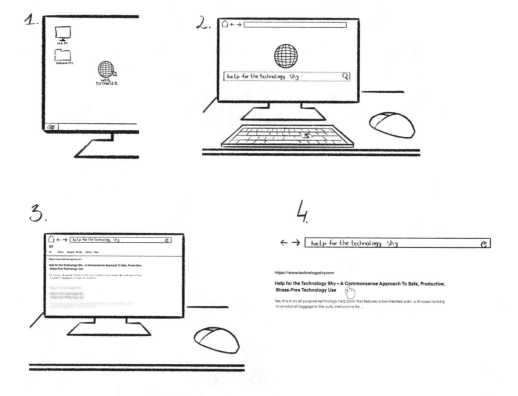

VISIT <u>WWW.TECHNOLOGYSHY.COM</u> FOR MORE TECH HELP (AND LOTS OF FUN STUFF)

"Slow and Steady Wins the Race"

Means: Hastily jumping into an activity, job, or something else can cause problems; often a more consistent approach, even if it is slower, can be ideal and give better results.

Tabby's Magic Formula for Productive, Stress-Free Technology Use

When it comes to technology use, it is important (if not downright essential) to have…

- clear objectives[1]
- a calm & focused mindset[2]
- careful documentation (e.g. this book)

---

[1] Michael Gorzka, *Help for the Technology Shy,*(Newton: Squirrels Drinking Coffee, 2020), 73–78.

[2] Gorzka, Michael. "The Power of Focus." *Help for the Technology Shy,* www.technologyshy.com/focus. Accessed 6 June 2020.

Technology Users Often Have to Wear Multiple Hats

1. Detective

Do you remember the NBC Sunday Mystery Movies in the 1970s? (Tabby doesn't but Tech Wizard Mike does!)

We can resolve technology mysteries through investigative practices which entail methodical research, talking to the right people[3] and taking notes.

---

[3] Gorzka, *Help for the Technology Shy*, 319-338.

2. Historian

Obsolete devices can be problematic and even unsafe to use.[4]

(So you need to know how old your devices are.)

---

[4] Gorzka, *Help for the Technology Shy*, 350-360, 334-338.

3. **Archeologist**

Sometimes you have to reconstruct the past.[5]

For example, you may have set up a device without transcribing or remembering which usernames and passwords you selected for certain things (such as device administration).

You would then need to methodically go about retrieving them or resetting them (help from customer support might be an option).

[5] Gorzka, Michael. "Forgotten Passwords." *Help for the Technology Shy*, www.technologyshy.com/forgotten. Accessed 6 June 2020.

4. **Archivist**

Organization, *clarity* and *documentation* are key to productive, stress-free technology use.

They will help you **take control** of your technology use.

How to Make the Purrfect Cup of Tea

We need to apply the same methodical and logical procedures we use to brew a nice cup of tea to our technology use.

1. Start with fresh, cold water.
2. Place a tea bag in your favorite cup or mug.
3. Bring water to a rolling boil and immediately pour over your tea bag.
4. Steep for 3 to 5 minutes.
5. Remove the tea bag.
6. Add milk & sugar.
7. Relax and enjoy!

Productive, stress-free technology use (like tea brewing) necessitates taking logical steps in the proper order to realize a *clearly visualized outcome*.

Drinking tea can help relieve stress and anxiety.[6] (Plus the tea brewing procedure itself can be quite relaxing.)

---

[6] Legg, Timothy. "Try This: 25 Teas to Relieve Stress and Anxiety." healthline, www.healthline.com/health/anxiety/tea-for-anxiety. Accessed 6 June 2020.

Things to Record in This Technology Notebook

1. Know what you are using.[7] For each device you own, look for and write down…

- the model name of your device
- the "software version" (or *operating system)* your device is running
- your device's *model number* and *serial number*

All roads lead to Rome from here. Knowing what you are using will be instrumental in getting *good help*.

Record this info for each of your devices.

---

[7] Gorzka, *Help for the Technology Shy*, 137-140.

You can *search* and/or *noodle around* for your device's "About" screen or window.[8]

Home Screen

[8] Gorzka, *Help for the Technology Shy*, 163-166.

2. Write down what you need to *login* to your devices…[9]

This could be a username & password combo, passcode, fingerprint, facial recognition, et al.

---

[9] Gorzka, *Help for the Technology Shy*, 144-145.

3. Write down what you need to *administer* your device (e.g. username, password and answers to security questions).

You may need your administrator login info to install new apps and to update your device's operating system.[10]

---

[10] Gorzka, *Help for the Technology Shy*, 92, 285.

4. Write down your *cloud account* info (e.g. username & password and cloud web address).

Cloud accounts can be accessed through a webpage **and/or** through an app on your device.[11]

---

[11] Gorzka, *Help for the Technology Shy*, 312-318.

5. Write down the web site addresses usernames & passwords and security questions for your financial accounts, online merchants and any other website that you need to login into[12] — including *email*.[13]

[12] Gorzka, Michael. "Wrangling website passwords." *Help for the Technology Shy*, www.technologyshy.com/wrangling. Accessed 6 September 2020.

[13] Gorzka, Michael. "Easy Email." Help for the Technology Shy, www.technologyshy.com/easyemail. Accessed 6 September 2020.

6. Time for a scavenger hunt![14]

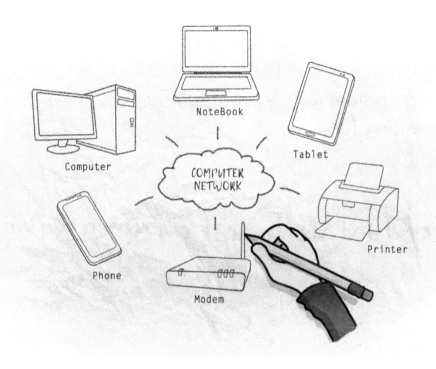

Are there any other devices (or "*hardware*") in your home?

If so, document them in this book (including model names, serial numbers and device purposes).

---

[14] Gorzka, Michael. "Technology Scavenger Hunt." *Help for the Technology Shy*, www.technologyshy.com/looksee. Accessed 6 September 2020.

If you have *Internet service* at home…

Write down the name of your *Internet service provider*, their website address and your login info — and list any of their equipment (e.g. a "router") that you have possession of.[15]

Careful and Methodical Documentation

[15] Gorzka, Michael. "Technology Scavenger Hunt." *Help for the Technology Shy*, www.technologyshy.com/scavengerhunt. Accessed 6 September 2020.

7. *Cellular service?*[16]

Find out (and record in this book) **how much** you are paying and **to whom** you are paying — and when your contract expires 🗒

[16] Gorzka, Michael. "Your Cellular Service." *Help for the Technology Shy*, www.technologyshy.com/cell. Accessed 6 September 2020.

Can you incur additional charges? If so, find out — and record in this book — exactly how that could happen.

TIP: Your local librarian may be able to assist you with customer service phone numbers.

It is important to keep on top of things.

Technology-related services are constantly changing and/or evolving —sometimes for the better and sometimes for the worse.

For example, Tech Wizard Mike was about to renew his cellular contract for $50 a month (🙀) when he found a another company which offered better service at a much lower monthly cost.

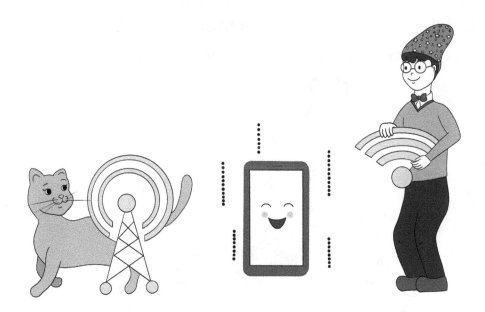

7. "Mystery charges"

A gentleman we will call "George" signed up for a **trial version** of a service on the recommendation of a friend and then forgot about it.

He took his eye off the technology ball, so to speak.

Six months later, George noticed the monthly charge. He had been paying $14.95 a month for nearly one year for a service he had not been using.

This gave George a clear **objective** which was to <u>stop</u> that monthly charge and (hopefully) have the prior payments refunded to him.

1. George *searched the web* for the company who had been automatically debiting his account.

2. He then searched the web again for that company's customer service contact info.

3. George explained his situation and the service was stopped and his payments were refunded (thankfully, the company was reputable.)

Tea Brewing
cooking directions

CLEAR GOAL, METHODICAL PROCEDURE & PATIENCE

Let's beee careful out there!

A key component to reaching productive, stress-free technology use is to have the info you need when you need it — hence this book.

But even though *Tabby Cat's Guide to Thoughtful Tea Drinking* is a passwords book in disguise (🫣), if you take this "tea drinking journal" outside your cloistered domicile, you will need to keep **very** close tabs on it.

What if I lose this book?

The short answer is: **Don't**.

IT IS VERY IMPORTANT TO KEEP YOUR EYE ON THE BALL
DURING TECHNOLOGY USE

"I lost my passwords book" tips
are available on the Help for the
Technology Shy website[17]

---

[17] www.technologyshy.com/lostbook

Rule of Thumbs (Rules of Thumb?) During Technology Use

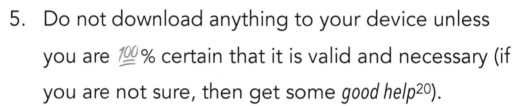

1. Proceed methodically with a clear objective (as in tea brewing).

2. *Breathe.*[18]

3. *Stop, look & think before you click or tap.*

4. Be especially wary about attachments[19]

5. Do not download anything to your device unless you are 💯% certain that it is valid and necessary (if you are not sure, then get some *good help*[20]).

6. Do not provide <u>any</u> personal information to someone you do not know and trust (while keeping in mind that anyone and anything can be *spoofed*).[21]

7. Watch out for scams; use *commonsense.*[22]

---

[18] Gorzka, Help for the Technology Shy, 35-36.

[19] Gorzka, Help for the Technology Shy, 194-195

[20] Gorzka, Help for the Technology Shy, 319-338.

[21] Gorzka, Help for the Technology Shy, 196-198.

[22] Gorzka, Help for the Technology Shy, 167-201.

Get free IPad and IPhone

Click here to claim your free

Conceptual Understanding

Yes, it is important to diligently document your technology milieu.

But it is equally important to <u>understand</u> what these things are actually for.

For example, many of Tech Wizard Mike's technology shy friends did not know the differences between…

- their device's *login info* (which could be touch ID, facial recognition or a username & password combo)
- **and** their device's *administration login info*
- **and** their *cloud account login info*[23]

23 Gorzka, Michael. "Different Logins." Help for the Technology Shy, www.technologyshy.com/logins. Accessed 3 September 2020.

"Stop, look and think before you click or tap" is a Help for the Technology Shy mantra.[24]

But in this book, we can add stop, look and think — and if necessary do some **research** — and perhaps write down whatever you are not sure about into this book.[25]

---

[24] Gorzka, Help for the Technology Shy, 191.

[25] Gorzka, Michael. "Setting up a new device." *Help for the Technology Shy*, www.technologyshy.com/newdevice. Accessed 6 June 2020.

Example Device Entry

Model Name: MacBook Air

Operating System: macOS Monterey

Serial Number: C02X54DOJHD2

Login password: hzlford1948+ (We can also login with fingerprint Touch ID)

Administrator username: techwizardmike@gmail.com

Administrator password: 38sKoool^1969

Example Cloud Account Entry

Web address: www.tabbyscloud.com

Username: techwizardmike@icloud.com

Password: Percent Cedar Jane Undivided

Note: We are sharing files & data (e.g. contacts and calendar events) between our notebook computer and smartphone thru our cloud service.

Example Website Entry

Web address: www.bankofusa.com

Username: tabbyscratch

password: eportx22#

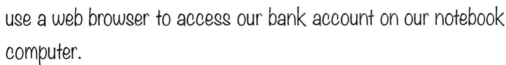

Note: There is a bank account app on our smartphone. But we have to use a web browser to access our bank account on our notebook computer.

Note: The Username & Password for bank of USA is saved on our notebook computer.

Tips for Creating Passwords

Passwords are...

"... a common form of authentication and are often the only barrier between you and your personal information. There are several programs attackers can use to help guess or crack passwords. By choosing good passwords and keeping them confidential, you can make it more difficult for an unauthorized person to access your information."[26]

---

[26] Cybersecurity & Infrastructure Security Agency. "Choosing and Protecting Passwords." https://us-cert.cisa.gov/ncas/tips/ST04-002. Accessed 22 August 2020.

A **strong password** consists of at least 10 characters and includes a combination of uppercase and lowercase letters, numbers, and symbols.

Do not use words that are in the dictionary.

Example: Northgatplaz1953$

A **unique password** is a password that is only used with one account.

So you would have a **different password** for every website you login into such as…

- email
- banking
- shopping
- medical
- insurance

Passphrases

Depending on the website or device, you may be able to use a just as **secure** (but easier on the eyes) passphrase.

A passphrase is simply a handful of normal words or phrases that would be easy for you to remember (and perhaps easy to sketch).[27]

rabbit, balloon, cloud, flower

FOUR RANDOM
COMMON WORDS

DIFFICULTY TO REMEMBER:
YOU'VE ALREADY
MEMORIZED IT

---

[27] Garcia, Mike. "Easy Ways to Build a Better P@$5w0rd." National Institute of Standards and Technology, www.technologyshy.com/passwordbook. Accessed 22 August 2020.

According to NIST guidance, you should consider using the longest password or passphrase permissible.

rainbow tree sad unicorn puddle ball

IF YOU ARE A VISUAL PERSON, SKETCH AWAY!

Tips for Creating Entries

- Remember slow and steady wins the race.
- *Breathe.*[28]
- Proceed methodically.
- Take the time to understand what each entry is for.[29]
- Write as neatly as possible.
- Remember that passwords are CaSE SeNSItIVe.
- Explanatory doodles are a bonus!

dancingtater4243^

(FITNESS MEMBERSHIP PASSWORD)

---

[28] Gorzka, Help for the Technology Shy, 35-36.

[29] Gorzka, Michael. "Clarity is Key." Help for the Technology Shy, www.technologyshy.com/clarity. Accessed 3 September 2020.

Clarity creates simplicity.

Create a separate entry...

- for each of your devices

- for each of your cloud services

- and for each website that requires a login (even if the login info is saved onto any of your devices)

USE YOUR DEVICES AND ONLINE SERVICES AS YOU WOULD BREW A NICE CUP OF TEA (I.E. THOUGHTFULLY, PATIENTLY AND METHODICALLY)

Tips for Using This Book

- Keep it within easy reach during technology use.
- Keep it up-to-date; erase out of date entries (or remove the page entirely)
- Review this book periodically. Make it your bedside reading until you feel $\underline{100}$% comfortable with your technology use.
- If you take this book outside your cloistered domicile, keep close tabs on it.

THINK POSITIVE!

Summary

Use this book to record…

- device info

- website logins

- technology-related goals

- "how do I…?" questions

- ideas for potential projects

- your favorite tea drinking experiences

- and any technology-related conundrums or kerfuffles
  you come across

Hey, There's More!

There are online tutorials and how-to videos to supplement everything we talk about in this book.

www.technologyshy.com

And there are additional Help for the Technology Shy books including "Help for the Technology Shy", "Your Technology Path to Follow" and "The Little Computer Help Book" plus some whimsical gratitude journals and our children's picture books.

You can visit your local library and/or adult community center and ask for assistance in getting to our humble abode on the Web. Once you're there, please feel free to reach out to us with any questions you may have.

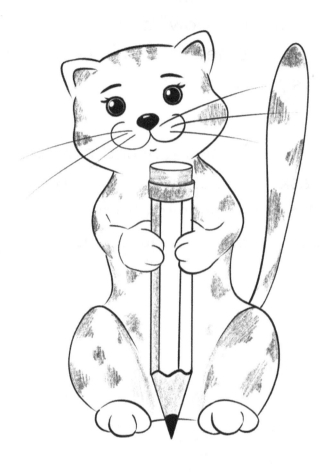

OK, YOu're ON! START wriTiNG!

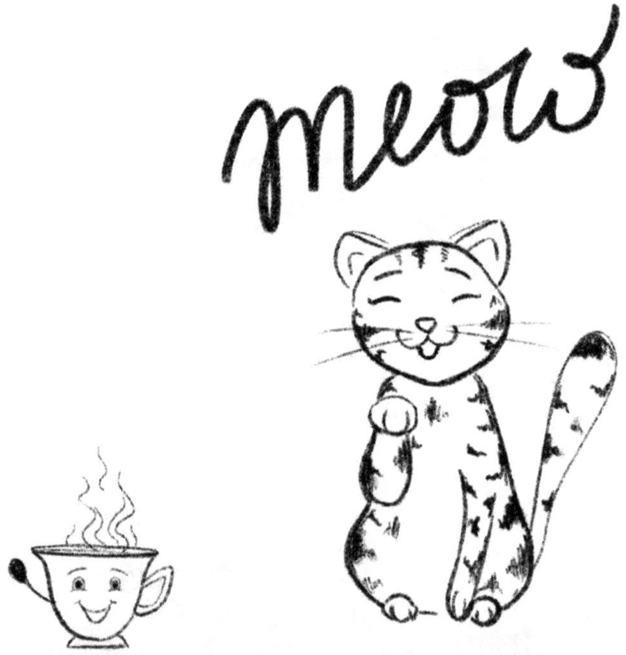
meow

www.ingramcontent.com/pod-product-compliance
Lightning Source LLC
Chambersburg PA
CBHW080535060326
40690CB00022B/5140